THE ORIGIN OF BALL PYTHON

There are 42 species of pythons in the family Pythonidae; the ball python is just one of 10 species in the genus Python, which is a sub-grouping within this family of reptiles. Pythons are a constrictor, which means they wrap their bodies around prey and squeeze until they suffocate. Ball pythons are one of the smallest of all pythons, and only grow to about 3 to 5 feet long.

Knowing and understanding a few basic ball python facts will help you decide if you would like to own one as a pet. The ball python can live to be up to 50 years old! They earned their name because they tend to curl up into a ball if they feel threatened, and they love to hide in dark places. They can make good pets, as they can be quite friendly with humans if handled often from a young age. However, make sure you consider all the facts before purchasing one of your own.

Common Name: Ball python or Royal python

Scientific Name: Python regius

Native Habitat: Western and Central Africa

Lifespan: With right care, they can live between 20-40 years antique.

Size: They will grow from three-6ft. Females are a good deal large in girth than males.

Expert Level: Great for beginners of every age.

Temperament: Baby Ball pythons are normally very shy and as they become old Ball pythons will become more engaging and curious.

Handling: Make positive to keep to handling your Ball python on a regular foundation in order that they end up used to human interaction.

HERE'S WHAT YOU WILL NEED TO CARE FOR YOUR NEW BALL PYTHON(S):

Enclosure: There are many distinctive ways to maintain a Ball python. The maximum popular way is to preserve your toddler Ball python in a fifteen-20 gallon terrarium. If you are seeking to become a breeder, check out purchasing a rack device. Rack structures are the exceptional manner to preserve medium to large collections of Ball pythons wherein you can connect Flex watt heat tape to proportion warmness.

*** In our opinion, child Ball pythons will experience more secure in case you begin them in an enclosure smaller than 25 gallons. Then, as your Ball python grows, cross ahead and boom the size of their enclosure. ***

A simply cool aspect to do in your Ball Python is to create a Bioactive Vivarium which includes developing a herbal dwelling area with plant life, substrate and residing organisms that act like a cleanup group in the enclosure.

HOUSING MULTIPLE BALL PYTHONS

Do not cohabit your Ball Pythons. Yes, some humans do correctly cohabit their snakes; however it isn't a good best at all. Your Ball pythons can turn out to be pressured out or injured. The most effective time you need to have snakes together is at some point of breeding.

Water Dish: Water is very important for your Ball python and need to be in their enclosure at all times. Make positive to NOT use distilled water on your reptile. If you do not recognize in case your tap water is safe, we might endorse the use of bottle water like spring water. Also, you could you the product: "ReptiSafe® water conditioner which is notable for water bowls and gets rid of chloramines and chlorine, detoxifies ammonia and nitrites, and provides vital ions and electrolytes which assist to hydrate newly received animals."

Substrate: Do not use sand or cedar substrate. Safe alternatives: Reptile Prime, Repti Bark and Newspaper/Paper Towel.

Hides: It is nice when you have hides, one on the recent facet and one on the cool side. Your Ball python could be able to effectively modify their temperature having a cover on both aspects.

I am certainly glad that we have had such wonderful remarks about our Reptile Prime substrate and I can without a doubt say it's miles one of the first-class substrates on the market to use for Ball pythons. If you are inquisitive about shopping a bag, please visit ReptilePrime.Com to place your order. The substrate is likewise to be had on Amazon Prime. Canadian customers are not able to buy via the internet site;

however they should buy thru
Amazon Prime.

HUMIDITY

Ball pythons on common need to have approximately 60% humidity of their enclosure. Babies once in a while need a bit higher. My non-public tip is that in case your Ball python has troubles dropping you can need to elevate your humidity barely. Just a few methods to add increase humidity: dampen bedding with a sprig bottle, larger water dish. Cover display top seventy five% with a towel, place a humidifier in the equal room, location a waterfall characteristic in the enclosure and adding stay flowers. Keep in thoughts if you stay in a place that receives bloodless and dry in the winter, it is probably subsequent to impossible to maintain the humidity excessive. Try your best to maintain it as close to 60% as feasible and refer to the losing segment if you need hints about stuck shed.

HYGROMETER

I am continually surprised how many keepers decide out of purchasing this very essential tool for preserving maximum reptiles. A hygrometer is a totally less expensive piece of equipment that permits you to measure the humidity on your reptile's enclosure.

Shedding: Ball pythons will shed their pores and skin a couple of instances via their existence. The more youthful the Ball Python is the greater frequently they'll shed. When your Ball python is ready to shed, their scales will appearance stupid and their eyes will start to look blue that's called Pre-ecdysiast. Sometimes for the duration of this era, your Ball python may additionally refuse to devour that's flawlessly regular. To assist your Ball python have a full shed, you may barely improve the humidity. When your Ball python sheds their skin that is referred to as Ecdysiast. You will see your Ball python begin to rub their little faces on decor, the terrarium, rocks or maybe you in case you are keeping them. If the humidity is correct and your python has no losing problems you should have a stunning complete shed.

Shedding Issues: If your Ball python has stuck shed, first ensure that your humidity is high sufficient in their enclosure. There are a few ways to help with caught shed is using a Rubbermaid or Sterility tub with holes. The first manner is to soak your Ball python approximately an inch of (simply hotter than room temperature) water for half-hour. The second manner you could help is through dampening a paper towel with heat water, twisting out the extra water and putting in a tub. Then, let your Ball python cruise round for 30 minutes to one hour. Once your Ball python has both soaked and cruised across the paper towel, placed on a rubber thumb to softly take away the stuck shed. If you be aware which you are not able to remove a watch cap or a piece of shed that appears proscribing, please visit a neighborhood breeder or vet to have it professionally eliminated.

Scale Rot: If you notice that your Ball python has a rash or blisters this will be scale rot. Scale rot is normally because of the humidity being manner too high. First, location your Ball python into a totally dry surroundings and we would recommend the use of paper towel as a substrate as you could trade it regularly to preserve the enclosure dry. Wait an afternoon or before putting a water dish lower back into their enclosure. Once you location a water dish lower back into the enclosure, in case you word that the water dish has spilled onto the paper towel please exchange it. Make sure to easy up without delay in case your snake has urinated or defecated. Finally, go to the vet so one can begin a course of antibiotics to assist heal your snake.

HEATING SOURCE:

Heating mat (under tank or facet), heat tape, ceramic heat emitters or a basking light. UVB mild now not required. The easiest and most efficient way to preserve a single Ball python is with a basking mild or under tank heating mat. This may be effortlessly purchased on-line. For large groups in a rack machine, Flex watt heat tape is a outstanding choice. You can locate this either on line or at a hardware store. Do you no longer use warmness rocks on your Ball python's enclosure as your python could get burned.

Temperature: Hot side need to be between 85-ninety one°F and must now not exceeding 93°F as it may start to kill energy for your Ball python. Cool aspect must be approximately 80°F.

Thermometer: In order to make sure that your temperatures are correct on your Ball python's enclosure, we trust it is a MUST to make sure to purchase at LEAST one. We surprisingly advocate buying so that you are able to measure the temps on both the hot and funky sides. There are many options in the marketplace. Shop round to see wherein the fine offers are. You also can purchase a Digital Infrared thermometer that reads the temperature immediately.

FEEDING:

We typically start all of our infant Ball pythons on live small grownup mice as soon as every week. Once they've commenced feeding often, we start to switch them over to frozen/thawed. You can maintain your Ball python on live or switch to frozen/thawed something works best for you. Please notice in case you feed stay you need to oversee the feedings as stay mice can injure your Ball python. The length of the prey has to be the same size as the largest a part of their frame. You can switch your Ball python over to rats whenever you feel love it. Normally, we wait until our Ball pythons are feeding on medium or massive person mice. If you're feeding live, try to find a neighborhood breeder in your location who resources rodents. If you're feeding frozen, there are numerous on-line businesses that deliver bulk mice and/or rats on your door. To prepare a frozen rodent, both thawed out in a single day on your counter or region in warm water to defrost. DO NOT MICROWAVE YOUR RODENTS. Once your Ball python has eaten do not keep them for twenty-four-forty eight hours.

Feeding Issues: Ball pythons are recognized for being choosy feeders, so do not right away experience like you're doing something wrong if your Ball python does no longer want to devour. If you have got a new child Ball python that has in no way taken a meal, they'll refuse to take food for some weeks as they are nonetheless complete from the egg. After that, in case your new child continues to be refusing to devour, you could need to help feed. If you have got never help fed earlier than, please try this with a expert. NEVER FORCE FEED YOUR BALL PYTHON.

If you have got a child Ball python refusing to devour from a breeder or save that has stated that they've already taken a few food, your Ball python may want some time to acclimate to their new environment. Also, double take a look at to ensure that your temperatures and humidity are accurate. Here are some different tips: try switching among stay or frozen rodents, slightly heat a thawed rodent a little greater in warm water, switching between rats and mice, attempt a smaller rodent, try feeding in the night or right earlier than bed and attempt feeding in a separate smaller feeding box. Keep in thoughts that if your infant Ball python is refusing to consume, please maintain your offerings among 1-2 weeks aside to keep your Ball python's feeding reaction sturdy.

We have heard of a few keepers providing a one of a kind color mouse, scenting the mouse and braining a frozen/thawed mouse. I haven't heard approximately a ton of keepers having success with the ones strategies, however it's far always well worth a attempt.

REGURGITATION:

Ball pythons are extremely touchy to regurgitation. If for anything purpose your Ball python regurgitates, ensure to wait approximately a 1.5 weeks earlier than feeding again and supply smaller food for approximately a month earlier than imparting a regular meal. If your Ball python regurgitates a second time, please visit a vet.

RESPIRATORY INFECTIONS (R.IS)

If your Ball python has signs of Respiratory contamination, please go to a vet to diagnose your snake and get hold of antibiotics to deal with the contamination. The faster which you go to the vet the faster the recovery time may be. Also, make the subsequent adjustments to their enclosure, keep the recent facet at 92°F and the humidity round 90%. A warm and humid environment will help the recovery manner. For minor RI, there's a few achievement with the usage of F10 veterinary disinfectant to nebulizer your snakes with. I might best endorse doing this in conjunction with having a vet take a look at out your python. If your Ball python has a bad respiratory contamination, ask your vet if they feel that they need to be off food for a time period.

Mite Prevention: Anytime you deliver a reptile in your property or collection, make certain that you quarantine them away from different reptiles. There is a product called Prevent-A-Mite that you may spray into their enclosure with a view to without a doubt do a wonderful job.

Mite Symptoms: If your Ball python is striking out of their water dish a lot and you see black specks floating round inside the water, you can have a snake with mites. Also, you could double test their scales to peer if there are any raised scales with mites hiding.

Mite Treatment: If you discover that your Ball python has mites, make certain to wash your Ball python in warm water about an inch deep. While your Ball python is bathing, completely disinfect their enclosure. In my opinion, I could get a separate like Rubbermaid/Sterile bathtub or terrarium and spray down with Prevent-A-Mite. Let the enclosure completely air dry and use paper towel as a substrate with nothing else within the enclosure. After a day or region the water dish back into the enclosure. You will want to continue to bathtub your Ball python, disinfecting your enclosure and use Prevent-A-Mite for about a month or so.

WHEN YOU ORDER A BALL PYTHON(S) FROM BHB REPTILES

Once you receive your Ball Python(s), please investigate your field and the python. If there are any problems, please call us for the duration of commercial enterprise hours or email us for the duration of non-commercial enterprise hours for the fastest service. If there are no troubles, please area your python at once into their new home and offer water. Wait to provide food till 5-7 days so one can permit their stomach to settle from transport. Finally, we would recommend extremely light handling or no dealing with the first week they arrive if you want to turn out to be acclimated to their new surroundings. Most of all, experience your new partner(s).

THE END

www.ingramcontent.com/pod-product-compliance
Lightning Source LLC
Chambersburg PA
CBHW060947130726
48001CB00003B/1105